James Liddy
Selected Poems

DUBLIN

UNESCO
City of Literature

James Liddy
Wexford, 1996

James Liddy

SELECTED POEMS

Edited and Introduced by John Redmond
with a Biographical Essay by Tyler Farrell

ARLEN
HOUSE

Selected Poems

is published in 2011 by
ARLEN HOUSE
42 Grange Abbey Road
Baldoyle
Dublin 13
Ireland
Phone/Fax: 353 86 8207617
Email: arlenhouse@gmail.com

Distributed internationally by
SYRACUSE UNIVERSITY PRESS
621 Skytop Road, Suite 110
Syracuse, NY 13244–5290
Phone: 315–443–5534/Fax: 315–443–5545
Email: supress@syr.edu

978–1–85132–026–4, paperback
978–1–85132–036–3, hardback

Typesetting ¦ Arlen House
Cover Image ¦ Paul Funge
Printing ¦ Brunswick Press, Dublin

CONTENTS

ACKNOWLEDGEMENTS

Special thanks to Jim Chapson without whose help and guidance this selection would not have been possible.

Acknowledgements are also due to the following publishers: Dolmen Press, White Rabbit Press, Capra Press, Malton Press, Kerr's Pinks, Blue Canary Press, International University Press, Creighton University Press, Salmon Poetry and Arlen House.

INTRODUCTION

John Redmond

Although highly valued by many, the poetry of James Liddy is hard to hold "in a single thought". There are a number of reasons for this. While many of his collections can be tough to track down, his relative neglect by literary criticism, and the consequent uncertainty about his place in the Irish canon, mean that some readers do not know what to look for – or even that they should look. There is also the question of geography. Just as major parts of the poet's life were split by the Atlantic, the same can be said about his readership. In 1966, as a junior but enthusiastic member of Dublin's literary scene, he "did a Joyce", heading to Spain, before settling for good in the United States. If his Irish audience was apt to lose track, in literary terms, of where he had gone, so his American audience may not have understood – quite – where he was from.

Liddy's critical reception has also been 'blurred' by his speed of production. He published a great deal, with various American and Irish publishers and in a wide range of formats: books, pamphlets, limited editions, niche anthologies. Much of his most striking work is contained in posthumous collections and many of his poems remain unpublished. A *Collected Poems* did appear in 1994, but this was just at the point when he began to write much of his best material.

To offset the bewildering abundance of his *oeuvre*, this book has been conceived in a selective spirit. The lay-out is mostly chronological, but not all of his books or pamphlets are represented (nothing is drawn, for example, from the juvenilia of *In a Blue Smoke*, his first book). Emphasising the latter part of his career, this selection aims to give a sense of how his career developed and of what kind of poet he became. It highlights his best work with the conviction that, for most purposes, good writing speaks for itself.

In making a case for the importance of Liddy's canon, one could promote it, convincingly enough, as an early example of the Americanisation of Irish literature, or, in a similar vein, as an early example of 'out' gay Irish poetry. Still, one should be careful. The favoured categories of literary criticism can sometimes drown the reality of the living, breathing artist. While such perspectives on his writing should not be neglected – they deserve elaboration from his critics – this book tries to shade his work from the glare of 'automatic' approaches. Liddy had an open, many-angled view of the world and his writing is best received in a similar spirit.

Although charm is one of life's great lubricants, it is also one of literature's great distortions. Liddy was certainly a charming man and his life did have its 'legendary' aspects – but it would be easy to over-romanticise him. The cartoon version of his biography (an Irish poet, during the Summer of Love, arrived in San Francisco, fell in love with the Beats, and flung off the shackles) could paint him too much as a 'Redskin', not enough as a 'Paleface'. In truth, he had little interest in "the barbaric yawp" and, when the mood struck, could be as fastidious and feline as James Merrill or Marianne Moore. If, in the words of Novalis, "chaos in the work of art should shimmer behind the veil of order", then Liddy, consciously, looked both ways, towards chaos *and* towards order. He was more Janus than Bacchus. As 'Blue Mountain' – the first poem in this book – demonstrates, he began in relatively formal vein and the hard-earned casualness of his later poetry came gradually.

Among the many effects, positive and negative, of Liddy's move to America in the mid-1960s was an attachment, manifest in his writing and conversation, to the pre-television Ireland he had left behind – this despite being a gay poet who had moved to a more tolerant culture. Having once belonged to Dublin's literary scene, Liddy was reluctant to let that scene die, even when it seemed long dead to others. His poems – his prose-poems especially – gossip eagerly about that half-forgotten past, dropping old-fashioned names as though they still carried their original cachet. The opening of his prose-poem 'Miles' gives the flavour:

> John Jordan said there are two kinds of dead. Pagan sensual dead satisfied as in the dream of Yeats and our dead: the church kind, soft decadent dead ... I drove him home from the T. B. Hospital over the hump-backed canal bridge, we passed by the booth. Michael and Hilton used to say I lived in a telephone kiosk.

But richly woven as this secondary world was, we should remember what it did *not* contain. A major part of his value, as poet and conversationalist, was that he had absorbed *nothing* from television. At times, the surprise of reading a Liddy poem is akin to meeting someone with an entirely novel set of household gods.

If some of his favourite themes – sex, religion, history – were not so surprising, his treatment of them usually was. Not so much an erotic poet as one who was in favour of eroticism, he was also a spiritual poet who had a lingering fascination with institutional religion. Popes, priests, and bishops frequently show up in the poems hinting at a life he might have lived:

> I that could have
> been a wonderful preacher
> became instead an amusing teacher –
> I thank God for mercy –
> — 'For Jeff, 1978'

He had too, a historically informed imagination, always looking to retrieve little-known facts from the past, piecing them together in new shapes. Far from being stuck in his age group, he – again – looked both ways, towards those who were much older and those who were much younger. Conversation between the generations is one of the electric currents of his work. As is often the way with enduring literature, looking back is a way of looking forward. If Liddy returned to personalities such as John Jordan, Elizabeth Bowen, and Austin Clarke, it was with an inkling that they might be waiting for us around the next corner – "When we dead white rabbits arise we will cook up literature again".

In his poem, 'The Skaters', John Ashbery (one of the Irishman's many admirers) somewhat humorously compared the range of a typical poet's experience to balloons floating in the air ("The more assorted they are, the/Vaster his experience"). There is no doubt that Liddy kept aloft a wide assortment of balloons, and this helps to explain why – despite a furious work-rate – his development was slow. Liddy's 'solar system' (to inflate the balloon analogy a little) contained a complex array of planets – 'Milwaukee', 'Homosexuality', 'Mother', Catholicism', 'Law', 'Clare', 'Teaching', and so on. Given the elliptical and widely-spaced orbits of some of these 'bodies', it is not surprising that it took him a long time to achieve a worthwhile alignment.

Liddy was a late developer but, unlike many other writers, he did not *stop* developing. Evidence that he wrote his best work in his last decade or so is contained in books like *I Only Know that I Love Strength in my Friends and Greatness* (2003), *On the Raft with Fr. Roseliep* (2006), *Askeaton Sequence* (2008), *Wexford and Arcady* (2008) plus his three posthumous collections, *Fest City* (2010), *It Swings from Side to Side* (2011) and *Rome That Heavenly Country* (2011). Individual pieces like 'Miles I-III', 'The Territory of The Planter and The Gael', and 'Cooking and Jack Spicer' highlight the strengths of this late style: intense insights about others, close attention to detail, wide range of reference, unexpected conclusions and sudden shifts of thought within agreeably unstable forms. There is nearly always a clear refusal to be sentimental. More than any other Irish writer that comes to mind, he took to heart Kavanagh's dictum that tragedy is underdeveloped comedy.

Liddy wears his major influences on his sleeve: Yeats, Baudelaire, Kavanagh, Rimbaud, Kerouac, Spicer are principal presences, but he read widely and absorbed much – one can find traces of Creeley, Bishop, O'Hara, even Lowell ('How Mother Came Home', for example, bears comparison with 'Sailing Home from Rapallo'). No doubt fortified by his reading of Beat literature, he employs, from time to time, a kind of elliptical shorthand, not so far removed from the late modernism of Brian Coffey and Denis Devlin. Private, or semi-private, references give weight and glamour to individual lines and are accompanied by a host of signature characteristics: name-dropping, obscure memories, provisional phrasing. He has a talent for parallelism, a device which has the benefit of tightening his many provisional forms:

> Luther put a nail on a church door
> Jesus had a nail put through him

> If I hold hands with you
> I hold hands with you
> blessed dream and shake
> If I hold both hands with you
> I hold both hands with you
> a shaken shade
> > – 'Et Nunc Manet in Te'

Liddy's gifts as a writer would also be gifts for a novelist or for a dramatist – his virtues in the main are not *purely* poetic (in the sense of mastery of the line-break, or facility with rhyme) and this directs us towards the genre in which, arguably, he has his greatest achievements: the prose-poem. Auden once said that, "form releases imagination" – and with Liddy this is especially true of *hybrid* form. The short piece, 'Note' (in *A Munster Song of Love and War*) is an early fore-runner of more elaborate successes in the genre like 'In the Cloud', 'Wunderbar', and 'Dream Cottages'. The prose-poem is, too, a feature of *Baudelaire's Bar Flowers*, a book attractively punctuated by a series of letters to Patrick MacNeice (a UCD maths lecturer who committed suicide around 1969). Showing his love of challenge, such epistolary experiments demonstrate how Liddy's 'I' is nearly always aimed at a 'Thou'. As much as the poems record encounters, they are also conceived *as* encounters.

In its hybridity and flexibility, its sincere uncertainty and cultivated mystery, Liddy's writing points toward a possible future for Irish poetry. Unlike the armour-plated lyric so prominent in recent years, his poems seem airily written, as if they were footnotes, afterthoughts, shavings from some larger writing project. One might even think of them as paratextual. "More than a sealed border or a boundary", Gerard Genette once wrote, "the paratext is rather a threshold". And this sense of being in the margins to something grander, a literary footnote, a preface, a signpost, is, for Liddy, not just a matter of biographical accident, of moving to Milwaukee, it is woven into his entire existential stance. Consistent with the great Emersonian tradition to which it is not so distantly related, and which Irish writers, from Kavanagh to Muldoon, have always found beguiling, poetry here is always "on the way". The arts, as Emerson put it, are initial, not final – it is where they aim, not where they arrive, which matters. Like thresholds through which the freshness blows, like architraves into the blue, Liddy's poems point beyond themselves to the rich diversity of life. Cathedrals, boys, bodies, books, food, adventures – always the pressure of a life being lived forces itself against the outlines of his verse. And, if a poem feeds into that energetic continuum, if, so to speak, its heart is in the right place, what matter if it *appears* modest or minor? A poem is only as good as where it goes.

from
Blue Mountain
(Dolmen, 1968)

BLUE MOUNTAIN

Blue mountains are of themselves blue mountains
And white clouds are of themselves white clouds
And there is a blue mountain, Croghan Kinsella,
And around it there are often white clouds.

Whether all things are accurately themselves
Or modifications of each other I do not know
But clear mornings from my bathroom window
I see white clouds and a blue mountain.

COOLGREANY

A corner of the sun –
Balanced by wires and a row of pruned apple trees
On a southward leaning hill –

A road fall-out that roofs a hundred souls –
Three-roomed cottages with attic – a handball alley '1927'–
Drinking fountains –

Beauty queens courting late –
A ninety year old cobbler still at work –
History's heavy hand –

The blackhatted crone who remembers hiding under
    the bridge
When the redcoats marched in to evict –
Bailiffs and battering ram –

Maud Gonne riding out on a white horse from Arklow –
Tolstoy speaking from a platform –
Now nothing more eventful than emigration

And not being on the main road hangs over this cliff of
    earth –
The sun piling on forgetful grass –
Village doors opening –

Old neighbours come out in Sunday best – like
Moths they drown in airy warm waves –
A Japanese cherry and a copper beech – back from the
    Street

The Doctor's residence –
Windowed in Virginia creeper – a curtained and

obscure Versailles –
In the dark somebody I know is kissing somebody –

THE REPUBLIC 1939

In the last village before the frontier
The refugees squatted down
To scrape a handful of earth of the Republic
Then, with that amulet, crossed.
The soil held more dearly than any baggage
Did not tend grey olive trees
Nor rose-coloured almonds nor green pines almost blue
But dried among the bric-a-brac
On mantelpieces of Peru and Mexico.

EL FERVOR DE PALMA
for Anthony Kerrigan

On another evening, when it is not easy
To hold together a religio sensually overflowing,
What is so laden out there with yellow
It fans the dusk to honey?

An Alexandrian mind overheats
Though in December lemon trees,
And down flights of long steps
A coming of twilight vendors.

EL FERVOR DE PALMA
for Elaine Kerrigan

It is warm and blue coming to Christmas.
Flowerpots on balconies bloom to sea.
Enredadera hangs its purple tangle
On walls, and smells of Wicklow.

To stay in a minor key is religious,
To pray a little within the self
And finding it not a temple
But a terrace of drowsy flora.

from
A Munster Song of Love and War
(White Rabbit Press, 1971)

1

The hounds can't
Come in
The steeds can't
Come in
He tries to come in
The music of the erotic chase sounds
But the cap on his yellow hair gets knocked
    on the floor.
Young men with yellow hair lift him over
    the furniture. Their tears
That want to come into the poem
Freeze inside love.

Note: I pointed to the picture of Collins on the wall. "Him," the intruder said, "my mother was his sister. What'll you have to drink? Come on, I am home on holidays from New York. I went there in 1952 but it was a diabolical metropolis then and it's still a diabolical metropolis." "Will you be going to Béal na Bláth?" I asked him. "Ah they're all hypocrites and if he had lived he would have gone after the lolly. My mother did and she was his sister – and why shouldn't I – I come from a family of cynics. But I tell you he put the English out of Ireland ... bring drink for them," he shouted to the barman. We started to move out. "Before you go I want to give you something else ... Here it is, Babóg." He kissed me.

from
Baudelaire's Bar Flowers
(Capra Press, 1975)

CORRESPONDENCES

Nature is a church where the pillars
Speak obscure words
Man travels it through a forest of symbols
Which spy on him familiarly

Like long echoes that fall
Into a sombre unity
Huge as the darkness big as the light
Perfumes colours and sounds answer each other

Some perfumes are as cool as the bodies of kids
Mellow as oboes green as the fields
Others are perverse opulent and corrupt

Expanding infinitely like amber
Music benzoin incense which sing
The paroxysms of intelligence and sensuality.

CORRESPONDENCES

Whatever it is it is the murmur of evil
It comes on like a soldier in a bar
Hearts are not had hearts are found
And you are chosen for the works of love.

It is not the love college kids pretend
It is not the brotherhood of soldiers it
    is soldiers
It was always this black mystery
Of you and a few others being chosen.

The beauty demons bring does not dry up
In fervid hearts of perverts lies The
    Church Daimonical
The opposite of wives the murmur of evil
The soldiers soldiers coming on.

CATS
for Cypher

Lovers in the afternoon or untenured teachers
When they are older and sit in draughts
Go crazy over sweet prowling cats
Nicer than kids in the house.

Friends of knowledge and special sex
In stillness and nocturnal terror
Erebus would have used them as touts
If they could have lost pride

They learn to understand the beautiful camping
Of the great sphinxes staring in the desert
Who pretend to have an unending dream.
Mystic pupils glowing with stars.

DEAR PADDY,

I know your decision and the poems connect. Three
weeks ago in this room you were reading *Les Fleurs du
Mal* while I listened to the Dáil debate on gun running.
I didn't discuss the poems with you though you asked
me. I would like to make up for that since you have
decided on your own to descend into Hell, where
most of these poems start from – where their light
shines from now with your light.

Gun running that Irish sport – forewarning you would
give up your physical life as the poet sacrifices his
energy. Baudelaire thought only the soldier, the poet, the
priest (the priest of Onan) were to be imitated. The life of
a poet like a perpetual morning after battle. Emotions
(especially rituals of dismissal) traced back. We barely
breathe in a hot house where fires of the poem shoot.
Mallarmé said Baudelaire was the poison we learn from,
"Always to be breathed though we die of it."

You bring pain and light in here. As the bridge. I cannot
say as the correspondent because you wrote no poems.
Your dying has brought parts of what you thought
(And what I and even Baudelaire were looking for) into
the poems. Maybe nothing more is happening than the
three of us have met in a bar where we know the
barmen and have decided evil redeems good. The way
you love best at your most masochistic.

I do not suggest I am less dead than you as I leave
these poems to rest for a while to see if they need
redefinition; though I know our hearts will not jump
at any airport when we see each other.
                              Love,
                                James

THE SUNSET OF THEM

The sun is Louis XIV exploding like an actor
Happy the asshole who enjoys making it
Without being conscious of how dumb he is.

I was at the party. I heard them talk
Poet on the circuit academic at the whiskey:
"You have articulated the new consciousness."

In vain I perused the Apollo of Reed
And the Dionysius of Dublin now Full Professor
O the high swishing of that cloak in Berkeley

Eyes out of Keats hair by Byron talk by Shelley–
Know the fat cat enemy in your own country
And be against the years at catching dollars.

from
Corca Bascinn
(Dolmen 1977)

Did you see the Jesus fish?
I didn't see the fish. Then you can't
    have your wish.
Did you throw a pebble with each round?
There are no pebbles above now on the
    ground.
We mess with saints, Paul, I mean spirits
Have an audience like them but what do they
    make?
Asking what grows in the pool is asking
What is the root of Jesus
    (underwater clings to something as
    Jesus clings to you)
Paul,
If a god does breathe in the pool?
I try to get dead drunk on the
Thousand hints of an absolute divinity.

It wasn't imagination friend to hear the banshee
   vowelling through her overcombed hair
   back of your ex-lover's flat

   (Wasn't imagination to have The Castle's
   puffy eye on vanishing Eire through the plane
   window hands sweating)

It wasn't imagination friend to see near Banana
   trees young prostitutes of both kinds
   dream of $50

Many sky-women through my public golden eyes
Much cloud-boys through golden eyes

Imagination don't get on a plane with me and be
   my friend

from
At the Grave of Father Sweetman
(Malton Press, 1984)

CROGHAN

There is a beautiful valley
of cows and small streams and some years
snow comes between Annagh and Croghan
a cabin with a half door and lots of children
in barefeet and strong farmers up lanes
and I and my young father (the new dispensary
doctor, the functionary who fills out
the medical supply forms at night) swinging through
in the car that's allowed petrol with the priest's
cap-doffing at each crossroads –
the social welfare Officer Mr. Weadick
sits in the back and on his lap
a pile of anonymous lined letters:
who's working who's malingering.
"I must investigate each complaint,"
as we pass Mrs. Cullen's up Ballyfad.
Does the valley stay beautiful when the peasants
trapped in it trap people as well as hares?
Where can the child go except to being boiled alive?

1943

WOODENBRIDGE GOLF CLUB

A quick nine holes
low small trees
fairways a narrow
lawn rain-drop shined.

Billiard grass, bunkers
like golden bathtubs,
desmesne trees under which
the ball flew like a pheasant.

Plus fours, holes in one
and the 19th hole was back
past the station to the hotel,
Major Binstead played host,

Mary Williams rang the yard
bell; time for her workers
and her to go for a drink:
a druid kindness fell

from the bottle –
I remember when golf
was Vespers evening prayer.
Light failed behind

trees on the Avoca river
the fish swam past boulders
for our supper,
I and my mother

in slacks were rapt
putting on the last green
what well being
the world was a cosy womb.

When the mist came down
from the valley hillocks
the fairies played golf
elfin and very smart.

from
A White Thought in White Shade:
New and Selected Poems
(Kerr's Pinks, 1987)

How Mother Came Home

Yeats and Pius XI had just passed away
so it would be a stranger world
but Ireland would be the same
in the shoreline the star of Palladius
hung somewhere and his saints still knelt.
There would be servants and nothing to do,
mother thought of reading and of romance
in a little singing country all secure:
Christ looks after Celtic larking hearts.
It would never be as gracious as the Plaza
Hotel but it certainly would do.
It crouched like a sea monster in the cosmic zoo.

In the early morning tender bumping out
From Cobh I felt nothing about barely remembered
parents but watched with intent the churn
of the dark water not yet glistened blue:
the slide and swell were rather terrifying
and how do the fish move in this froth
and billow, how can they survive?
I'm a chubby little chisler not very bright
shall I learn to swim like Daddy and to dive:
living is not the crock of gold my maid says it
is (she lies) but just a crock of shit
there's no way I'm going to fit.

Then they waved and came down
the gangway smiling and one held out
the love that fucks the heart day in day out
and that with passion winds raves the mind.
She gave me a blue cellophaned basket of
fruit from New York and a pale yellow
bunny (my first friend Billy),
The Goddess pure and in fur coat stole

the psychic places growing girls should find
(my emotions will never now be trite).
Beauty is strange as a secret woody mole.
From that day forth Mother has been bright.

POSTCARD TO JIMIN IN MANCHURIA

The first rule in writing postcards is:
include the names of four poets. The second:
don't make it sound like a poem by Robert Bly.
He think Yeats was a Lutheran. No evangelical
deep image, here. And name four places.

Postcards travel like confetti near the China
beaches. They blow into California, they come
into my hands like birds; like winter birds
who can warble anywhere. Our confetti comes
from China, as Wallace Stevens says; blowing
westwards like folk smoke. This morning your
card of Tiger Beach: is that its name or is it
a translation? Whichever, looking at it, it
has cliffs like Kilkee. This morning, my card
of cliffs to you that used to see as far as
New York, that now behold Cathay!

There are no trees on these heights to protect
birds – to find song you have to lift it out of
the sea. You set up on the sheer rock with
confetti made from spray and seal sound. The
folk warble of a wedding westwards to Tiger
Beach. My singing postcard: Anti-Evangelical
pro-sealing Fate.

James

from
In the Slovak Bowling Alley
(Blue Canary Press, 1990)

These people are bowling, these people are living. I watch them "bowl," the snob I am saying "how pathetic." But in all actuality these people don't care if you've read the latest Kerouac novel, they don't care if you wear polyester, they don't care if you don't drink imported beers. They're here to be with "people." (Whether those people are like them or completely opposite them.) They are enjoying life, regardless of what people think of them. Pure pleasure.

I see fat old women – who haven't laughed since their Honeymoon – laughing, I see studly old men whom no one (female) has given a second glance to – being studly. I see young sexy women – being crude and unsexy – yet being their sexiest. People are themselves. Genuine. "Yet he who is genuine isn't"

The majority of the bar is looking at me, staring, pointing, talking about me. The feeling of joy, to bring some external stimuli to this lovely "hell hole"/ pleasure dome. Thinking "they either wish they could be me (young – good-looking – healthy – fresh) or hoping to beat the living crap out of this freak (young freak – dirty pot smoker – general piece of shit)." If I can give either of these feelings to these lovely souls who long for energy – rejuvenation – just "a general kick in the ass" it would be my supreme intention at this moment.

I would like to bring up one type of person I fail to mention out of pure ecstasy, the pregnant bowler – bowler with one in the oven. I feel as though when this "very very very young bowler" is born he would be able to bowl on his own.

Think of it – every time his mother approaches the line she thinks: "knees bend, head steady, relaxed grasp on the ball – step, step, step release (ball) – elbow straight – follow through." As this mother "bowls" the infant also bowls. The mother and young one are connected, they should both be feeling the same thing. If only that young young bowler could remember the technique he could be truly happy his whole life.

from
Art Is Not for Grownups
(The Blue Canary Press and Kerr's Pinks, 1990)

I

Love

The last cloud to pass
into the bonfire of St. John's Eve.

XIV

Remembering How They Stood

Where's the Big House, Pat?
It's in the Lawrence collection, Sir.

XXVI

Outside Lady Gregory's Garden

Carve your beloved names in mud.

XXXII

Art is Not for Grownups
in memoriam S. B.

He took silence into his heart
So he became near-silent.

L

Wisconsin

The high school band was legendary.

LVI

See-Through

Yeats is the Hemingway of Ireland
You can see through the hair on his chest.

LXXX

MLA in Washington D.C. III
At the tomb of Woodrow Wilson, National Cathedral

A crusader with puppies at his feet
hush-puppies on his feet
in his hands a League of Nations shield
in his heart a croquet mallet.

from
Trees Warmer than Green:
Notes towards a Video of Avondale House
(International University Press, 1991)

LITTLE SONG FOR IVY DAY, 1991

The countryside a long vaguely troubled sleep
shot by bird-song, we'll go to the hotel to drown it:

there is not in this dry world
a hostelry so sweet as the Vale View
where friends murmur to friends
and their bright glasses meet.

A man is softly singing the
original of "The Dawning of the Day"
rescuing it–lead kindly sound–
from Van Morrison's deep throat.

A toast to Arklow, his stones
in the Rock his soul up the hill
of Main Street like a burning drill
in the pavement where a spit crucified.

If I was the blackbird of Avondale I would
sing down the river of Aungier Street dreams
the grey-white stones of the house would flow
on the water, the trees warmer than green.

from
'She is Far from the Land: Poems 1989–1993'
Collected Poems
(Creighton University Press, 1994)

'THE SAADIANS, MARBLE, TILE, AND FLOWER'

Small spurts of green, flowers like lavender,
large forget-me-nots, hundreds of dwarf palms.
The sprinkle of peace in the garden
beyond the horseshoe arches of
the Mihrab carpets. Flowers around
tombs. The guide in Fez
says they are "serviteurs," in fact
princesses of princesses.

The Kashbah Mosque, deep ochre,
olive trees steady everywhere.
There is no God but God and Mohammed
is married – praise to God as
I repeat the prayers of rosewater heaven,
stalactites ... for building a rendezvous,
a "date-house" for the dead.

White pillars under the painted horseshoes
cool, a tool for knowing dream-death,
Under the shadowy walls mother
of petal in the garden with her class
the well-aired fortunettes.
The tombs a second invitation:
a pale willow a silver poplar
the single cypress sounding in the sky.

Prince princess in high ochre enclosure:
share the resurrection from the sick.
In the mountains none of this happens
the seven spheres plunge without illumination
the columns of glory without a break
each court person needs peacefulness
that after perusal becomes an island.

Pearl on tile dew of death in a sweet
hidden way indulged from view.
Yes, choose the point of the soul
that can linger on the zellig-covered
colours (where death-in-life is generous),
lying out in the open
outside secondary princes,
children maybe whom Exit clad
in the earth robes of the garden.

Over a basin with green tiled roof
yellow bills of blackbirds coo
solitary tree green ladder into space.
Plumbago slicing along wall
greyish-blue or violet tongues
a broader bluer flower of a boxed
shrub the path circles around,
roses down the side not near the tombs
stems leaves delicate unreal shades
prospecting the alternative beauty
the artificial ... salmon-coloured roses,
a burst of purple in a few bushes.

Out of vast redness red tower
of the Koutoubia, range after range of
the snow-covered Atlases,
blue sky on evening tide will turn
yellow at the base orange in the middle.
Snow music the muzzein's microphoned
fireword doesn't disturb the scents,
the tiles go in different directions
at angles or into diamond cards.

You did not accomplish works of peace
yet you entered and left a holy garden.

A long-billed stork flies in,
a nest on royal palace chimney.
The mountains are built of crystal rather than rock.
Surfeited with rosemary, no foreigner to luxury,
Mother your soul carried beyond the wall.

April 1987, Marrakesh

Last Light in Clare's Mind

It has rained like showers of arrows
a warm day in the yard. Pansy clips
up the drive for dinner, the red Fiat
muddy before the shed. Come let's sit
in the sun on the white garden seat
under a pear tree; Clare's wearing
a black dressing gown with
faded gold buttons. Big trees drowse
beyond the Dairy wall. Wind performs
a small peacock on pear boughs.
The wings of the angel of death
have a soft landing, no glaring.
The notes of Chopin etudes on the piano
reply from the study window,
the golden cocker spaniels "Ginger" and
"Mi Wadi" materialise. Buzz of insect summer.
A last setting outside the kitchen door
and death shall have its Scotch and soda.

The Mass priest says: Jesus is no magician.
He whispers in no one's ears, he works
through people. So it is but this morning
he whispered in both our ears:
I shall officiate right here.

TRANSLATE INTO LATIN FOR MY EPITAPH

He wanted his potatoes carried through the streets
by someone beautiful who yawned.

John Jordan said there are two kinds of dead. Pagan
sensual dead satisfied as in the dream of Yeats and our
dead: the church kind, soft decadent dead ... I drove
him home from the T. B. Hospital over the hump-
backed canal bridge, we passed by the booth. Michael
and Hilton used to say I lived in a telephone kiosk.

I invited John to convalesce over a weekend. He put
on his hacking clothes, he was very proud of them, he
mentioned them on each premises. He was staying in
the country. He was an old very tall angel ... He got in
the way of the dart players – did not notice. He said, I
demand to be taken to Mass. In the night he ranged
through the house, gliding into the snoring bedrooms,
suddenly awake. He stood on the landing, he looked
down the stairs, I demand a glass of milk. He lay in
the grey room in the morning; John it's time for Mass.
The gaunt deacon in bed smiled, Child, bring me a
large brandy.

We went by the back route, the slate quarry road, to
the Woodenbridge Hotel. He said he was a Roman
Catholic. You see Child, I enjoy doing it, it becomes a
sin. Gives too much pleasure, it is unlawful. Anyway,
God does not like it.

He said he had been to the Woodenbridge Hotel
before ... that fertile literary valley, at its start the tree
of Tommy Moore still singing, at its end Major
Bayley's hill where a wife gathered spinach for Frank
O'Connor's dinner. John had gone there with Paddy
Swift. They had read *Ulysses* together. In that
champagne text, liberation, a kiss. In that barn it was
bliss to win.

Back to Dublin, that imitation metropolis, an
imitation of Port Royal. A Port Royal, as it were, with

yellow hair near a railway station. Sean O'Sullivan, big, rosy cheeks raspy voice whispered to any gentleman who sat on the stool near him, Shall I compare thee to a summer's day, thou art more lovely and more temperate. He murmured to Paddy Kavanagh who looked into his Scotch.

John in the evening phoned from the pub Pius XII and Dwight Eisenhower, both eminently telepublic, being elegant monsters of the old school.

John started saying what Paddy said, It's a black day for me, consumption has no pity on blue eyes and yellow hair.

John wobbled on his wonky legs over to where you were sitting. In the name of God, pet. In the name of God.

Is it true, John, that the line from Terence that everybody quotes, *nihil humani a me alienum puto*, is uttered ironically by a slave?

Absolutement, pet.

He is elegant in Mount Jerome, not very far away from friend and fellow-petal Edward Longford. Spongy meadow, forest of flowers ex-Flanders and elsewhere. The flowers are bedded.

MILES II

My father had the contract for supplying shoes
to all the theatres in Dublin, in Jimmy O'Dea's
time. One day Mac Liammoir came to the shop, he
wanted white lace boots. Now my father had lace
boots all right, but no white pair. Will I ever
forget it, Jimmy? I was only about fifteen years
of age but I set to work, painting the boots.
At that time Mac Liammoir and Edwards lived on the
top of a house in Dawson Street. I remember the
stairs, it was peeling and dismal. I made my way
up and knocked on the door a long time.

Mac Liammoir opened it, took the boots; he didn't
ask me in. Jimmy, he spoke beautiful English,
didn't he? You don't hear English like that
nowadays, no, not at all.

MILES III

January 22, 1982

Dear Katherine,

The impetus for this letter comes from meeting the Beat poet Gregory Corso last night. Immediately we met he hived on to Paddy who said he was "very sharp." "Kavanagh knew he was a poet so he could sit with whom he liked. O he was a good man, a good poet." He also mentioned Brian Higgins (whoever mentions shoe-water-logged Brian anymore?). "Poor fuckers, they made a mistake, they bit the dust, but I'm alive." He talked about the Queen's Elm, and going with Paddy and Brian to the owner's house after hours, "Those guys owned that man, I'm sure they never paid him, their credit was bigger than his bank account, I'm sure."

Corso kept on praising Paddy, until taken off to the smoke pit by my students.

By any chance, were you present at these occasions? You probably had to get up for work the next day. I asked Corso to write a few lines on P. K., but he listens to so much Mozart he mightn't get around to it.

Katherine, I do hope you'll get better very quickly, and we must have a nice summer.

Love, James

from
Gold Set Dancing
(Salmon, 2000)

GOLD SET DANCING

It's the figures in the set, what they do,
how they execute their wins and weave
they come a little closer than you imagine,
how they start being great friends
thanking/being thanked for attentions.
The walls belong to them and me.

The feeling I had in 1940-something
hurtling out of the Paramount cinema
having heard Delia Murphy singing,
how a whole country could empty its throat.
I would move with boys-in-dreams through
that landscape, shawls, spinning wheels, masts,
a band of soldiers including myself.

For me at the beginning,
never a towered elite hermit,
the gold of Ireland did seduce
then I arrived in gold rush
town San Fransisco;
mouths, limbs, kiss-talking,
I replaced home mind,
emigrated to god and play.
I burnt love down to the ground
then we lay there.
Dancing starts again, the ground
is lustrous, all gold leaf.

Happy those stepping on the floor.
If I, woman and man
as my poetry mouth suggests
a sweep from both sides,
take the dancers' hands and kiss them
their ringed fingers turn to gold.

I find now I'm in a set with you
(I'm in love with a man who's just married)
whose movements elaborate ...
Your sense of operations your midnight colour
unalterable by heat or moisture.

FOR JEFF, 1978

I inherited my failure
from father
and married it to poetry
but came too fast.
I was superfluous
amongst the most dearly loved.
I learnt at last:
contemplate desired bodies,
Eros fires the mind
even more powerfully.
Honour – what is that –
it has at least nothing to do with sex
Honour is to love the friends that last.

I that could have
been a wonderful preacher
became instead an amusing teacher –
I thank God for mercy –
and went to many parties
to the same bar over and over
with the sweetest of drinking companions.
I visit the house of my mother
her big back garden/rose garden.

Rose petals are souls of the dead.
I reset you with neck and mouth
kisses like no tomorrow.

WHAT I BELIEVE IN ABOUT MEN

Leave Jesus and the Catholic Church to one side
for a few moments, then merge them with
what's below.

There is just one thing a man has to be
and that is a princess. The word "fairy"
can be used but only in Ireland has it
the right soul meaning. A princess does
everything for the sake of what it is
sparkle for sparkle's sake, depth charge
for depth charge's sake – hanging out his spirit
jewelry on the sun's or bar's clothes-lines.
Decorative glow. Observe the male of the womb
marching towards summer's exit. The point:
Jewelry is flesh and blood and shines for
no eyes but your eyes, morning noon and night.

from
*I Only Know that I Love Strength
in My Friends and Greatness*
(Arlen House, 2003)

DANS LA VOITURE ROUGE DANS LE STATIONNEMENT

In car dark I propose
the veneration of images
the divination of images on paper
also adherence to non-images

besides I'm inefficient and awkward
in saying anything
a little shy even after drink
and you're worse than me

My compliment to you
you're as good a drunken driver as I used be

God make a star
out of each of us
on the front seats
in the sky on the page
just in a sentence
say stars in just
a footnote say that's us

C'est moi began writing so beautifully in the 1870's
that poetry became C'est moi even if it wasn't as
beautiful. But it did better than before. It became a list
of lovers, if not quite that it stuttered as a list of drinks.
There are two sailor suits in this story and they were
never worn on the same day or in the same navy. One
was worn on the Seine and on the Thames.

Miss Enid wore hers walking down the main street in
Roundstone, Galway. Jesus, Mary, and Enid. The little
roads of the heart bracing itself for the gypsy frying
pan.

This would be the winter of Moi's fretting about his
vials in Africa.

Miss Enid walked in Connaught free of horrors, a
woman in a sailor suit, hurt as a woman a long time in
a pigmy Anglo-Irish West.

Moi stepping in company of nomads to their wells.

In Sommerville Miss Enid stayed in bed as she hasn't a
change of underwear, a lady's child.

I see them both taking a glass of champagne the colour
of the first plaster statue they prayed to. They never
interviewed each other except in imaginary transepts.

The beautiful product and the saleswoman of beauty.
The sales talk. Publishers flogged the books.

But Moi and Miss Enid wear sailor suits for beauty not work. Tightrope for beauty not exercise.

Moi whispers at last, "Under an African sun Apollo reminisces".

This caper concerns "blossoming and dancing", we
    want to see
the dancers in the dance. Partner Elizabeth Bowen
and Medbh McGuckian on the floor. Asking them,
invite McGuckian in the daylight, approach
Bowen at night, she's tabooed, she's in the speakeasy.
"As long as I can remember I've been extremely
    conscious
of being Irish ... I must say it's a highly disturbing
    emotion".
It takes an Irish person to know how difficult it is to be
    Irish.
She held up a varnished nail at the UCD English
    Literature Society,
"For years I used to go down the stairs to a London
    basement
and scratch on the window, Virginia Woolf admitted
    me to conversation".
By night in Dublin she put on red lipstick, wore a red
    dress.
Bowen like Jane in *The World of Love* was "tense with
suspended dew; her own beautiful restlessness was
    everywhere".
The aroma of desire, catalogued by Patricia Coughlan,
    fades in and out
out of her text. The meaning of *The World of
    Love* is – well – love.
The whimsical extraordinary set of moments
in *The Planter and the Gael*. Innumerable
word-strewn cries,
first half of a Bowen novel is hard then wonderful
    pages turn into
dewy driveways through grounds, with rereads
constant inspection of syntax image McGuckian

begins to clear.

One tries to recuperate from the Anglos

the other defies the Anglo-Ulster set. I dream in North
Cork

of a book written by a she, I dream in the North of a
poem without an I.

I am alien and Dionysian and in my books my house is
jammed

with lovers. I am alien primitive and Dionysian and
my poems

curate portrait galleries where nude lovers flourish.

My men are drawing-room sparks, my men march in
the doom-mist

of sublime revolt. I feel a sort of influence in the air

like the flame of a candle burning on saints' days,

my signature is as vibrational as parish flowers.

McGuckian deciphers until the morning, this is the
reborn country,

these are her dance steps: gone former syntax present
the ruin

of the narrative present sighs and ghost spakes.

McGuckian dedicates *Selected Poems* to Roger Casement

and the rebel Bowen declares when Mr. Churchill goes
I go. Floor eyes

around the clock. White poppies (war) white feathers
(cowardice) diamond bullets

(aristocracy rebellion) milordless (gentry gentillity
wealth sex)

secret hand (dried sweet hard tears), marry dancers as
they are.

Both writers people of the god and the goat

spikers of epics about solicitation as much as
salvation. People

of the harp Janus-like facing both ways to the harp
shaped graves

in briars and grass. Miss Welty on Bowen: Terra firma

implies the edge of the cliff. Miss Bowen Ms
   McGuckian,
take each other's waist as dandies and dervishes.
Otherwise no galas de jour for Ireland.
Dance we must, dance we have to, even in circles like
   this.

THE CABALA

The good cardinals
return to Catullus and Livy because they are stopped
at every Christian exit by slippered bureaucrats;
a consolation to a cardinal in old age is the sensual
dominance of poetry, the godlike chatter of great
    history.

In the sunlit garden of Wilder's they read and read.
The muses are people they discover, not all of them
    dead.
They don't want Horace's word only, they want to see
someone, the old age of cardinals is a glass in
    another's hand.

Meanwhile in the palace, there is no time for poems,
    they were
writing Encyclicals in less than punchy Latin. Our
    Lady
of Fatima waves her robe in the gardens, she also
    comes
to breakfast in the Pontiff's room. They talk science.

The cardinals who are not obsessive about *The Eclogues*
become toadies eavesdropping at the morning meal.
The Girl in the room and The Pope worry about
    Russia;
Cardinal Spellman will have to take care of it.

Cardinal Schuster, who got too few votes to be Pope,
    who
tried to get Mussolini sanctuary, runs the anti-court in
    Milan
(Martini now). He puts on the Mask of Ovid and gazes
at the river. Cardinal Tisserant studies Coptic texts,

holds a sword underneath for the day he will descend
as Cardinal Deacon and tap Pacelli's skull.

Through universal science, honeycombs, and birettas
Pacelli still walks quicker than anyone in procession of
    lace.
He barks on a golden telephone, "kneeling,
    Monsignor?"
Finally the Caesars are ladies, intelligent, tall, cranky.

The good cardinals still dream of poems that move
    like magi
or dolls. They think of the sighs of Jesus's donkey.
They wish they composed a poem that would start,
"Holy Father, pray for old rabbis, Max Jacob,
the sisters of Kafka, the prince and princess
of Hesse ... Holy Father, go to the slaughterhouses and
    pray".

The cardinals who feel they could sit on a donkey's
    back
place Catullus's page beside a fourth glass of wine.
They look up and catch a glimpse of St. Peter's:
Oh, Gehenna, Gehenna!

Miss Byrne in the Post Office
sent each year a birthday card
to Pius XII, Vatican City. She showed it
to me for spelling and punctuation.

from
On the Raft with Fr. Roseliep
(Arlen House, 2006)

BLACK HAWK ISLAND
9/17/05 to Jonathan Williams

She liked the Enlightenment
she liked cabbage.

What America needs
is not more cars in
church parking lots
but in a rural setting
a non-Christian poet.

(Lorine's bio)
no kiss from Louis
careerless.

I was officially loved
by some in the world
thus not without merit
but disdain for others
was tornado-dark.

The waltz was lovely
not slow, danceable and
sprayable on water.

Migration to Club 26
supper club of pirates
bathtub gin makers
toy boys free rounds!

AR CHREAG I LÁR NA FARRAIGE

In the middle of the Ocean

Fishing in the summer, painting in the autumn,
    fucking
winters, gorgeous island.

Their hearts were fine in the wild winds, not writers,
    painters.

They would go into the waves, kick the fish to the pier or
    rocks.

If you went too far and started drowning they wouldn't
    help, the sea
was taking you back.

They knew Derek Hill's cottage on the hill was stacked
    with liquor,
their spoils as liberators.

Toasts to the King of the island.

Women, what women, they were like men.

When islanders married they stayed with father mother
    brother and sister,
they weren't like Christian people, the Parish Priest got
    cross said no
to the keys to the school for a social, there was no hall.

The girls walked from one end of the place to the other
    remembering songs,
wanting attention.

The boys walked from one end of the place to the other
    remembering songs,
wanting attention.

Shaky sweet voices on the outskirts of revelation.

Tory, in one way or another, knelt a high priest.

On Cooking & Jack Spicer

Graham Mackintosh came to Milwaukee on a later
train because his cab had a crash on the way to Union
Station in Chicago; one cabbie was black the other
Arab and, though there was no damage, they argued.

This was Graham's first visit to the Midwest, though
his father worked in California for General Mills.
Graham was the second White Rabbit, after Joe Dunn,
and devoted his printing life as a publisher to the poet
Jack Spicer. He has done work for New Directions,
and does the printing for Black Sparrow Press, for
John Martin, including the Bukowski volumes. He
said Bukowski was a nice man away from his
publisher and fans, but an overrated drunk.

Seeing the essence of poetry outside the epic is brevity,
even if a repeated brevity, Graham said the important
thing about Spicer is he wrote short poems, short
books, short letters. 'Jack never wanted to be boring.'
'Early in life Jack had coffee with a little brandy, later
brandy with some coffee.' Spicer never got a job in an
English Department because he refused to do a PhD
under Jo Miles; she blackballed him. He worked under
David Read on the Linguistic Atlas of California; he
finished that. He would have some lettuce and a roll
for lunch. 'In the Berkeley Cafeteria you could hear his
tray shake as he carried it to the table.'

'He suffered from night blindness and many other ills,
all symptoms of alcoholism.'

'Wild Tony Aste from Salt Lake City or Larry Kearney brooding New York Irish had similar status. Jack didn't flirt, he wooed.'

His friend Robert Berg, the San Francisco librarian, had two fifths of gin every night and always got to work. State has an incredible collection of books on food, for many only the wrappers, texts taken home by Berg. 'John Ryan hid two quarts of gin in Berg's oven to stop him drinking; Berg came home with Naomi Frost a faghag; he couldn't find anything to drink but they started cooking: there was a huge explosion. John could never figure out what he did wrong.'

Spicer edited Brautigan's *Trout Fishing in America*; Brautigan really thought he was going to win the Nobel Prize. He was also broke. 'At his divorce hearing his lawyer was convincing the judge how poor Brautigan was, how badly his books were going. Richard jumped up and said his books were selling all over the world. He went broke, his Japanese wife took everything.'

'Wally Hedrik was important for me at CSFA and maybe for Spicer too, that's where I met Jack. Wally was in Gallery 6, the offshoot, with John Ryan. Wally went to Paris and learned to cook, that was how to get on in San Francisco. He made those small machine sculptures all his life. He was a nice guy, anyway everyone wanted a black friend. He lived with Jay DeFeo and gave a party for her 30th birthday. She promised to take her sweater off and she did. That is nothing nowadays but then.'

'George Stanley a la Joyce refused to take communion at his brother's ordination to the priesthood. So they hid him in a crowd of nuns who had received the host at an early morning mass. They stayed there in a block; no one noticed George was not in the crowd going to the altar.'

'Jim Alexander and a friend would go to a department store every Saturday to try on bikinis with the help of friendly clerks.'

These are the lives of the poets. Transparencies. When we dead white rabbits arise we will cook up literature again.

from
Askeaton Sequence
(Arlen House, 2008)

NOW

Say we walked in a garden, was it towards a picnic,
the banks of flowers were tricky so securely seductive
it was a long day with evening in it, there were people
but no picnic, it came after All Souls Day, it was
    heaven
in the rich complicated way the blessed have, we were
adults we were children we bumped along, say we
    were
talking facing each other we held hands, say our
    hands
turned to gold and the gold began spreading over our
bodies, no it did not smell like a perfume it was a new
skin, it was yes flesh in heaven, say it is off the
    freeway now.

Et Nunc Manet in Te

Luther put a nail on a church door
Jesus had a nail put through him

If I hold hands with you
I hold hands with you
blessed dream and shake
If I hold both hands with you
I hold both hands with you
a shaken shade
If I meet you once a week
I meet you once a week
If you say 'look at the moon'
I gaze at the moon
it holds out a cup of poems
If I have lunch with you
I have lunch with you
with stories of leprechauns
in golf courses' rough
If my line of talk is deep Plato
or Dionysius stay in reverie
If I put my hand on your heart
your heart beats like a plane
over Jerusalem a train in Oz
or I hold it in a cup with
a shaky banquet hand
I'm on a Seminary tour of the
planets or Dante touring a
vineyard's renewal of lovers
Your eyes are Pilsner pools
I'm a Central European alcoholic
If you come out of the blue air
I pick a song an air for you
This garden is not remembrance
it's a fire brigade in a fire

You half know what a fling is
I half know what a fling is
we don't care
If our lips salute they salute
at a crossroads our mouths wander
if they meet purgatory will go on fire
stars were tired yesterday but today
there is a clown prince called love
handing out music sheets
and here's the circus parade
stark sincerity on its high wire
our voices and eyes high up
we have been commanded
we have been wired
and now I remain in you

Nail on the cross sweet brew

from
Wexford and Arcady
(Arlen House, 2008)

HAPPY EASTER

Why do we call last Friday good, because on this day
there was a supper party, first of a few.

For liturgical reasons I'm thinking of Austin Clarke,
apostate, I hardly ever think of him. I remember in his
autobiography he talks of doing the seven churches on
Maundy Thursday around Dublin, where there were
flowers though it was the sad season, I suppose.
Indulgences? I did them with my aunt Gertie from
Donnybrook to Rathgar, I think Austin and I had
several churches in common specially Tranquilla
Convent upper Rathmines Road (polished floor of the
Carmelites).

A little volume for my birthday, does my sex life need
this kind of advertisement? Dear Jesus Christ, you alone
look beautiful you alone should have wild parties. Will
friends write little ditties for me?

Re Celtic/Anglo-Irish Eden/Arcadia that was childhood
with Clare Maggie and Josie in the house bitter very
sweet society, after it you had to find a common
dancing area between church and body.

I remember being in a bar with Austin after the Living
Art Exhibition opening and saying to him and Nora,
'With the changes in the Council you will be trekking
back?' Austin was old, 'I will consider that much later'.
Donagh MacDonagh and Nuala were sitting with us
smoking cigarettes, I thought of the Fourth Eclogue,
desinet ac toto surget gens aurea mundo/casta fave Lucina ...'
I imagined Austin again, 'No'.

Me though – never able to hang up the party's shoes.

CHRISTMAS EVE
for Sheila Roberts

The wife putting a candle in the midst of a holly
wreath, and placing it in the dining room window, said,
'The windows of East Clare are lighted up tonight in
case the Holy Family has nowhere to stay'. Under the
starred tree opening presents we'll be late for Mass,
we're always the family late for Mass, but then the
Doctor was different, half an atheist maybe but not his
wife. Then we'd go to a party, at the local lawyer's, and
the Doctor, maybe for the first time in the year would
go on the batter, and there'd be ructions. He'd have
scoops of gin, be as moldy as Lord Iveagh. Would we
get safely home the three miles to the house, without
being put out on the side of the road and walking over
the snow? We arrived for the ham, turkey, spiced beef
from granny in Limerick, Heidsieck, brandy lighted on
the plum pudding brandy butter by it. We wore party
hats at the table and pulled crackers, now more than
one adult was langers, this time the American wife, and
one or both of them would soon exit slamming the
door. If we were unlucky this happened before the
King's Speech at three o'clock, George VI with his
stammer out of an old German Bible.

MAY, QUEEN OF INCH

They were all after May, bank clerks, creamery
     managers,
Aidan Mernagh was crazy about her.
They'd go on spins down to the beach. She had a red
     Citroën.
She had an album of her boyfriends, she'd laugh over it.

The Byrnes employed May in the Post Office, their sons
     got a car
and toured all Ireland. They gambled, male madness of
     summer.
Everyone went bankrupt in those days, their father
     wouldn't.
'I'll pay my debts, a pound for a pound. The children
     can go
to America and get a start'.

Across the road, the O'Brien-Hennessys bought the
     pub.
American accents. They brought their old grandmother
     from
New Ross, black coat and pipe. She used to sit in the
     evening
after ten in the window.

May went up three quarters of a mile to her Post Office
in Coolgreany. She did Children's allowances, Radio
     licenses,
savings accounts. She took out her stamp collection or
the minutes of the evicted tenants of the Brooks Estate
(up to 1932). She brought down the album of her old
     boyfriends
and laughed over it.

Glossy photos that revealed the doctors who are knights of Columbanus, the singers supported by the knights, Richard King's mildly 1890s Celtic church paintings purchased by the knights, the bog cotton of the 1950s.

The heavy *Capuchin Annual* you'd think you'd need a forklift to hold it up.

The singer who was the printer said, 'The editor's brown robes with cord in the Gresham Lounge: Fr. Senan stood out in contrast to Peadar O'Donnell a suburban lapsed Catholic. Their table piled high with cakes. Their magazines seemed to eat them. I had a few of the cakes myself so I ended up printing the Annual which included driving Fr. Senan around. He'd want to go here, he'd want to go there, he'd come down to Wexford to look at the proofs, that would take several days, I looked after him. I drove him back to Dublin once with my aunt English, we had to stop at the Montrose for a meal, I never saw a man for the eating like that. Then he wanted to go to the Phoenix Park, I said I had to go back to Wexford. I left him somewhere on Sandymount Road in what looked like a derelict house, it was in the dark the windows broken. Maybe he wanted me to feel bad. Did you know he was expelled from the Order when the whole thing blew up? He was sent to Australia like Fr. Albert and the other Capuchins who brought the host to the condemned men of 1916. Father Gerard came round and asked how much is owed for printing most of the back issues, it was paid weekly after that, I tell you never work for the Catholic Church, there will always be a discount. He was one of the Magi alright'.

from
Fest City
(Arlen House, 2010)

Days with John Ashbery. A monumental exercise in
definitions. Place this screed between the pages of
your Douay Bible. Let this be on your desk like a vase
of flowers. Then you can select how to go about, how
not to go about, *amor* and *poesía*.

I

An Indian student who said he was from Lucknow
came up to Ashbery. The poet opened two buttons on
the student's shirt to remark, "Look now, pay later".
In the crush of Axel's bar we broke up necking
between him and a student who said he had slept with
Allen. The latter milk fresh from the Seminary was
intent on hattricking celebrity poets in one calendar
month. The next evening, Wednesday, after Ashbery
Bombayed in T. J. Brubakers autographing his art
essay in *Newsweek* with what was in his glass, we
walked across Downer Avenue to a classroom where
he was to preside over Milwaukee writers reading
their work. Soon he fell asleep in front of them and
snored peacefully. Woken up we climbed to the
Kenwood Inn where he took a fancy to my friend
Tommy whose tight pants he loudly noticed. They
began to embrace. Later Tommy sat in Axel's weeping,
"I'm an ordinary guy from Oshkosh, why O why am I
so heterosexual when the most famous poet in the
world is trying to make me". Later more tears,
"Ashbery has asked me to go to New York to be his
secretary, I don't know what to do". I heard another
student tell the poet, "I have to give you a bad kiss
compared to what I give girls".

II

In Dublin Ashbery lunched in The Old Stand and I
think sang a few songs from Victor Herbert. He and
his friend David had come from Portugal, the air
conditioning hadn't worked in Oporto but the poet
commented, "There is always our friend the martini".
He ordered salmon, Paul asked him to sit for a portrait
and offered to give a tour of the gay bars. He
demurred, "I am often bored in such places". John told
a story before he left to pose for Paul in the studio. "I
met Philip Levine who told me he had done an
interview. Levine met Bly who said to him, 'I hear you
said nice things about me'. Levine, 'I said nice things
and not so nice things'. 'What are the not so nice
things?' 'Well I said that you and Gary Snyder were
good poets at the beginning, but then you knew how
poetry was written and your work went down'. Bly
said, 'Yes, that's true about Snyder'".

This was what I was going to add when you had to go
  back to your Supervisor.

I was talking with the Virgin Mary and she asked if I
  needed a lawyer to advise
me on domestic matters. I thought for a moment,
  maybe she's a lawyer as she
comes from a good Jewish family. She saw my
  thought, smiled, and said she
was a poet. She writes in Hebrew and English. She
  said to me, "Whey aren't you
nice to Jeff on the phone, he's a poet too", but she was
  joking again (thank God
for that). So now I put an imaginary blue (Mary's
  colour) envelope around this.

from
It Swings from Side to Side
(Arlen House, 2011)

FRUITFULNESS

I lay there in my mother
as bad a Catholic as her,
they drove back from Dublin
they listened in the car
to foreign radio stations.

A fetus warped enough
to be a medieval fortune hunter
vowed to ineluctable things
blessing itself purging itself,
beseeching attention,
pre-disposed to drink as much as her.

Afterwards the close bosom
of a maturing mother,
warmer days and nights on the radio.
The foreign quality of our adventure from the start.

Anatole France, "The only honest man to emerge
during the war was Karl of Austria; but he was a saint
and nobody listened to him".

At four he sold fruit and plants from his child's garden
to help those on the streets, put his wardrobe out on
the street. His great uncle gave him the Order of The
Golden Fleece; reading it he remarked the rules were
out of date and impossible.

Ate meat only at breakfast, denied himself alcohol for
duration of the war only a warm mineral for his heart,
no death penalty for deserters or even mutineers,
commuting death sentences on Czech radicals by
Austrian courts martial, no bombing of cities by his
planes.

Against the U boat campaign (if the Americans come
in there will be no Kapuzinergruft Capuchins), against
Lenin going home in a sealed train (he told the Kaiser
that it was unfair to the Russian people).

Joseph Roth, "We could easily demonstrate from
Germany's history since Luther that there was an
entirely organic, natural, even self-evident progression
by way of Frederick II, Bismarck, and Wilhelm to
Hitler ..."

So Schönbrunn November 1918. Shivered by the heat
from the great porcelain stoves everyone rushed from
room to room. Admiral Horthy, shivering, tears, "I
will never rest until I have restored your Majesty to
your thrones in Vienna and Budapest". Princess

Melaine Metternich, 86, "Tell his Majesty not to worry, revolutions come and go". They go in six cars.

Eckartsau March 1919. Hunting lodge in deep wooded meadow, shooting in the woods for dinner.

Solo dash disguised to Budapest to claim from Horthy The Regent. Karl, "You swore an oath to me", H, "That is no longer valid, it's been superseded". K, "I have released no officer from his oath. And you are also bound to me by a second and more personal oath – that of a court official". H, "Give me a few weeks".

Second dash with Zita in a private plane seated right at the back behind the wings over the Bavarian Alps, stalled at a railway station.

Where will the British dump them, Malta, Ascension Island, Madeira?

Up in Monte it's damp, no electric light smoking green wood in the fireplace, fungus on the chapel wall, a day's walk down, can't afford ox carts or cars, Karl walks down with Otto and Adelheid to buy toys for Karl Ludwig he's four, refuses a coat when someone runs up with one on the way back, chill mist in the trees, pneumonia turpentine camphor and caffeine injections plasters of linseed with mustard bags, oxygen fetched from the hospital.

Too weak to lift the Crucifix the boy Otto brought him.

"Ave Maria gratia plena ... Unser täglich Brot gieb uns heute ... The November manifesto is null and void since I was forced into it, no man can take away from me that I am the crowned King of Hungary ... Let's go home ..."

In Monte cafes in the Square, steps up gardens to the church accordions of Funchal, but a Capuchin brother with a crucifix?

Prayer above Funchal

Out of it comes the sublime. I want the sublime. There exists no other measure or stress.

A South African taxi driver took us up a mess of lush hilly roads to a tabernacle worked in silver over the altar sheltering a small cloaked statue, I am a shepherd I am a shepherdess.

Nossa senhora, speak to me in English (English is an illusion of the sublime). She is speaking in Crown of Stars English, she is speaking through each star.

Did she speak to you in English? Silver English? In Summer, in Monte?

Fleadhs are simple events. The business gets done. I am curious to know what happened on any day.

The ice cream parlour (not factory) brimmed with music lovers, new pot smokers, McDaid's entire crew. The ice cream disappeared as soon as you entered... A temple of the arts at this moment. Outside a Guinness heir in an Aran sweater asked the crowd, "Are there any good people who can change a hundred pound note for me?" Through the door came Tom Kinsella and Eleanor, the owled second best poet in the country. Leland Bardwell ambled through to the trestles in the backyard. The country's first poet entered groaning. Nods over craters and chasms. Tom inquired what were we having? Paddy was instant, "I wouldn't take a drink from an upstart like you". The rest of us got what we ordered (we knew who had won that round).

The scene drifted to anarchy, orgy... Paddy sitting on the kerb talking to a few children. I invited people to the house and there were musicians playing through my parents' rooms (they were in Kilkee). Soon to be famous performers roamed. Do I remember the name of a young Leo Ransome? Paddy didn't show up as he threatened (in his next column in *The Farmers Journal* he wrote I had turned him away from my door like a dog).

Breakfast time in town, the Main Street was littered with shape-filled sleeping bags. A funeral passed down the street, it was Mrs. Peters, the owner of the Railway Hotel. People woke to say it was the biggest funeral they had ever attended. Paddy came from somewhere, still standing. "Take me out of this fucking kip to Dublin". I wheeled the car round. The poet pissed several times under trees on the road, the last one before The Beehive. On the Bray bypass, Paddy groaned again, "Take me back to Gorey". A limit has been reached. I'm no longer Apollo's chauffeur or powder puff, "Paddy, it's time to get out of the car". The poet complied and shuffled off down the street towards The Dargle Tavern.

Driving is long, art is short.

Festivals are from Athens, poets from Sparta.

Dionysius is absolute, Bacchus is morose.

VACATIONS FOR CHILDREN

Children think of pitchforks. Holidays become
assaults on the young. There is car, road, map, two
opposing views in the front seat. Never lean forward
much to listen.

A place. Irish road uneven and bumpy uncompetitive
with hedges that loom high nothing visible except an
occasional cow other side of a field gate.

Front seat male titan on tillage. Patches of potatoes
and vegetables out the window.

This is across your country.

Specially the country of the female one.

She found Ireland in New York years ago and keeps
the details. Porridge tales in the morning, richer
evening plates in the evening, the invitation reads, we
are a clever talented people; we were victims so
spiritually aware.

A Goddess in her own right but with a husband.

Seeing the countryside out of the car window.

A new idea, see the country. An invention of this
summer.

The children were used to where they had to go.
Summers had been strangely Anglo.

White ocean blanket over rocks. Spray tugged, the
Anglo-Irish flora sparkled in return. The stone mouth

of George III across the Bay spewed foam at high tide. The villa was built with the boards of a coffin ship the Edmund sinking in sight of the shore (one imagines the pennies of the evicted poor sinking in to the waves).

Children tried to locate a legend, in what room in the 1880s had the whiskered Poet Laureate, the afternoon-tea-mad Tennyson, consumed tea with the Ross Lewin women? Our villa their summer place away from a Shannonside mansion.

The male had his way, the children should see something different. Under her influence they may be turning elegant.

Take them to the country. Show them Achill.

He was the kind of male who thought the family should go driving on Sunday. The female thought they should go a distance, look down a valley, find the public house.

They got into the car and went there.

They had to buy into the Garden of Ireland Program.

"Achill", the map said. Different from what you know. Incandescent near isle reached by a long bridge. She saw a bar at its entrance. She asked for a gin lime and soda. And ice. The publican had never heard of ice. The children learned the standing of ice.

Puzzled children. This was the West, few trees, stone walls, irregular fields. But were not fields larger, trunks leafier? Steeper paths to endless coves and beaches not so many rocks, purple violet haze. Amethystine. Turquoise. Greenish-blue landscape, wild flower patterns.

A word the children thought of "lush". The Lord is my lushful bride.

Diamonds in the waiting water.

Why did the cliffs suggest avatars? A sort of Last Judgment without pain?

Return to Anglos.

The Keel hotel was run by an efficient young Scottish couple. On a mountain above the street stood another hotel owned by Major Freyer. They drove up to it in the car.

Out on the lawn a crowd of young men in costume with bells on their hands and maybe on their toes. Morris dancers, the children's first and last. Their feet skimmed the hillside earth as if it was an English village green.

DREAM COTTAGES

The cottage was not just children it was the love house
the slave house of affection, which they attained after
they had spent time scouring hedge and forest for
places to merge themselves unseen. The rain had
fallen on them so often washing out their touching,
they knew very well what a roof was. The possession
of the cottage was the ritual of the covenant, they
could lie together surrounded in whatever little space
by the coming of children's voices. So we – they – lay
fairly quietly for the course of centuries. Then the
modern: houses and money. The West cottages, small
stone walls, wells, and goats, which had pretended to
be asleep now contrived to sit up awake.

Galway was just coming out of the cottage or the back
street hovel stage. There were houses, rooms, people
were painting them. They had floor space and nooks
for intimacies so began the huge era of decoration. The
bars too became larger emporiums, lounges added to
their front areas. But some of the bars tended to
resemble cottages, not only because people tended to
return to them, inhabit them, but also because love's
sorcery was practiced there. The Saw Doctors, frenzied
and restrained, brought it back with their melancholy
and fun by Lake Michigan. (La Fête Irlandaise
stretched up the lake, they could be heard in the
distance.) Someone started discussing their refrain
about a "Michael D". Several asked who was this
"Michael D?" Dave Brannan said, "Didn't you know
him, I used to hear you talking about him". "O Jesus,
yes".

Galway, wild oats. Kelehan's pub at summer's start:
fires getting heaped up with coal in the room facing

the hospital, retired R.I.C. men with poitín in upstairs rooms, the cider room at the back for the freaks. Drinks for the police after closing. Mrs. Kelehan would let us stay in the bar if she wanted to go on an errand, we were on the honour system to pay for what we took; the four of us, Michael D, dizzy scattered lecturer in sociology and politician, Brian young Professor of Classics to whom Catullus came in a frenzy after a few, Jim who had come with me from San Francisco a poet temporarily entwined with alcohol and I in residence for a year teaching Lecky and Yeats. We would put the afternoon away like children who wanted to stick around. Jim and I when young were Bohemians but we paid for our drinks. We did, the evening had to grow younger ...

I have to add Jim and I liked a young man whom we called Nora though that was not an accurate personal description. I also add the March moon reigned full. Nora and Jim were discussing the pub and Jim defined it, "This place is like a mental hospital, it's divided into doctors' nurses' and patients' quarters". Nora used to think Jim favoured the patients' quarters at the rear of the pub. We moved freely between the different quarters. Nora had a friend Dorothea who preferred the doctors' quarters that faced the ugly regional hospital across the street. This institution and Kelehan's had an intimate relationship as the pub was the local joy-in-death house, brothel and wake house. The sepia tinted oval framed portraits looked down on the strange group of sinners below.

We were coming to an end of a few hours academic drinking. Michael D entered frazzled carrying a suitcase. He opened it, took out a thick large notebook covered with his writing, "I've just come from the hospital after a short stay and I've written a lot of poems, I'd like to read them to you". I knew he did not mean the hospital across the street. Page by page his whispy voice took over conversation; the hour was here to make our return journey down the Corca Baiscinn coast. Jim had been sitting uneasily in his chair as Michael D intoned; when he paused Dorothea gushed over Jim, Nora was gazing more than a little love sick at Jim. James and Michael D concentrated on Lorca, the far away martyr with green eyes. They fell to the Republican pros and Falangist cons of the Granada event; debate broke out of what led to it; James had read Ian Gibson's *The Death of Lorca* and trumped Michael D, who made a bet James was wrong.

Michael D threatened to read, James began the shuffle out the door, Jim asked Nora, "Will you come to Clare, will you come down to George Fitzpatrick's?" "Yes". Dorothea knew from the moment that she had lost whatever complex game the three were playing. She interjected tragic foreboding her eyes. "Nora, do you have to go?" "Yes". Michael D. "And you're going to leave me in the middle of my reading". We were going down the pavement to the car, the shout hits us, "I'll follow you down to Kilkee and make you listen". We took to the eerie magic coast road in twilight past the castle that fell at the Lisbon earthquake, the bridge rocks and seaweed of Quilty with music blasting out of Casey's pub, to George Fitzpatrick's ultimate two roomed cottage of latest nights, dancers battering on the Liscannor flag floor, and George's cheerful malice floating in whiskey.

We had ordered when Michael D flew in through the door carrying the suitcase with the poems. We shuddered back to the piano and the walls. The customers recognised him from TV. With half hearts we invited him back to the West End house, elegant mid-century Victorian cottage. Party developed, we messed around, Nora and Jim in a corner, Michael D cranky as I produced the Gibson book. Trouble was more than a ghost in the air and I thought I'd leave the complex three together. I heard murmurs then shouts; I peered out the bedroom window and beheld Jim rolling and kicking a sack-like Michael D down the front steps. Standing on the road he lets out roars that could be heard across the Bay at George's Head, "Dirty fucking yank I'll have your head: I'm a member of the Parliament of this country and I have influence. I'll get you deported from this jurisdiction". We went inside as he drove off in the morning light and discovered his case; besides the manuscript a load of drugs for the relief of many kinds of mental pain and suffering.

APOTHEGMS

Deal with it, the light in which you might be good.

Blue dawn under Tree light, branches of poems.

Birth and death count but love stronger and warmer.

I got to know how to write sentences (I told others), do
not keep sentences isolated.

Kavanagh said the leaves that fall in Kensington
    Gardens
are universal leaves, why I have thought of this at the
last moment.

The Tree of poems at the beginning of Creation was in you
so you defended what it is to write a poem, (joined in a
minor way, Pound, Kavanagh, Spicer, Wieners,
    Niedecker).

It's right to fall in love if it gives you more
    compassion.

The Lord sent angels late, beautiful friends, I will not
name them as they might lose their wings.

15 October 2008

from
Rome That Heavenly Country
(Arlen House, 2011)

SEASON'S COMPLIMENTS

L'Arbre de Noel

The tinseled tree danced tenderly with me
through the night at the Cana Club
I knew I had a high ranking one in my arms.

The tree with its Magdalene hands
performed the passing out dance and the kissing
    dance
I knew the music was alcohol I held the parade kick
of James Joyce the alto shuffle of James Stephens.

I tangoed the tree down to the basement
I kissed it I said it was more my buddy than Jesus
it was as if I met the friend I had before marriage.
Were there Christmas trees before the electric switch?
Yes the hearth was worship and cemetery of trees.

A Druid at Christmas

Our literature is or used to be the priesthood
responsible administering the religion
of our place somewhere else. I am the spokesperson
for the "country under ours", the spells and
seduction chamber music of that third estate
in spasms chorusing from standing stones, raths.

Above us Latin trembled on the balcony, the
Holy Father wore Pilate's merciful eyes which were
made of emeralds. That antiphon from Rome but I
    gaze
under it at our fading first country of poisoned wells

and rock pools, nothing but quarries, Cuchulain drives
an accelerating bulldozer past the Hill of Tara.

I play carols on the piano adorned in a collar of gold
in the music I take my ancient tree (that northern light)
remodeled to Rome and place it at the foot of the
    Cross
where Vergil's shepherds provide provenance,
we're full partners in Domus Aurea's champagne.

Christmas I thought mother's not around
then there will be no real drinking.
The dead drive round in my bed-night mind
sometimes they rent cars or maybe they buy them.
My family was never righteous
they can't suffer changes of heart.
Star leads us down the valley of pines to paradise
    bulbs
pining for melody and mediocrity
I like the student who is nuts about baseball
and gets the bus to the stadium
and the one who lives in the suburbs
and composes poems about his mom.
I am the mother and father of bachelor parties
and it doesn't bother me there is a mother
in Christianity and no wife.

I thought of the Christmases
before these tinseled trees
I thought of the Masses before there were Malls
I listen to Music in bed that's the night mind.

I dream at Christmas of liberation
of Abe Lincoln
(who was our first President
our first war President)
taking a brandy tastefully
signing the Proclamation.

Next morning in the class
a black man is wearing
a blue ribbon that reads
"Membership in the NAACP".

An older white woman
gamely asks, "What is
the NAACP?"
He looks intensely at her.

Jolly Vatican 2

I've had my first drink of the day, it's after Cinderella
    Hour
I've taken the cup and sang "For he's a jolly good
    fellow"
under my breath. Part of my faith is at the supper
    Jesus set up
a restaurant and bar and trained to be the bartender
    (The Church
interrupted service for a long while but it has been
    relicensed).

IN THE CLOUD

I put my head in the cloud
I was touched by it
I said I must write about that cloud.

Immediately there appears the son. The father and son
    dance begins.
I know him, I don't know him.

Jesus meets and merges with the fishermen. He is not
    like "the doctors".
Still dark, he rises, leaves the house, to the open
    countryside. Before
dawn to the country light (those spaces).

He withdraws towards the sea, goes to the hills,
    through the cornfields,
the emphasis is on the disciples, having friends
    around, maybe bridegrooms.

The boat is in a storm, the waves obey, he awakes, "If
    the dead arise
from the dead the living can escape from the family.
    The Son of God is
disengaged from family, it is not quite about this.
    Think as much
about ghosts as about sex or children".

When he was walking on the water they thought he
    was a ghost.
A ghost is always coming towards us, until we are
    ghosts.

He seeks to remain unrecognised.

Garments turn into snow and words say, take up that
  shitty piece of wood,
as if the cross turns into a snow shower. Put black
  roses on the cross.

What happens? "This generation" never happens.

Jesus's promises: 100 burning houses, 100 lost brothers
  or distant sisters,
persecution or the persecution complex.

Jesus's commands bring up the question: seduction
  and conversion merge.
Perhaps we may take seduction where we can. We
  can't change the divine mind,
maybe we can revise it. The other query, shall we dead
  awaken? Get with
sacrificial persons, like Edith Stein or Berryman. I
  speak as an ancient Catholic
and so does Richard Rodriguez, "Catholicism,
  specially the Irish and Mexican
versions that shaped me, always took seriously the
  implications of Good Friday –
life is suffering. Whereas Protestantism seems to be
  centered on the Easter promise –
you can be born again".

Be practical, if arrested words will come like sleep.

The Son of Man gathers his elect. Bet they are not
  those who "teach like doctors".

Pretend you're not teaching, hide you're writing an
  essay on love ...

Bet Jesus talked about art and beauty when his friend
    Mary was criticised
pouring costly spikenard. Bet he thought, this is a
    wonderful thing that
is happening to me.

Bet he'd hang around the Vatican Museum.

Treat yourself to being reserved, love equals
    breakdown.

At the supper the couches are in place with the
    glasses. The apostles drink
in part because they know they have to deal with the
    horror of betrayal

(Wine in heaven, the father washes away the jeers
    from his son's face).

To empty yourself of divine certitude: that kind of
    drinking.

What is there? Jesus, his father and mother. What is
    real? Bridegroom,
brother, sister, some form of sweetheart.

When the friends desert him, the bridegroom in a
    white linen sheet shadows
him. Sunekolouthei … Wrapped in white.

Witness; nakedness; uncertainty; memory.

First love idea is best love idea.

On his deathbed, Charles Olson, "There are holy
    things, but nobody knows
they are holy".

The cup of wine in Jesus's mind.

Join hands. The church transmits this narrative. The
    story in the Gospels can not
be confined to the Gospels. How many of them did
    Jesus write?

There is this one.

St. Mark

ASK

Jesus as a psychiatrist knew how to play demons.
Not the point.
The Gospels are not reality TV.
they're partly
the teaching stories of the early Church.
Jesus can be the Rabbi
of severity, it's a teacher's ploy.
My students say, "Are you testing me?"
"I test you when I feel like it".
The woman had spunk, attitude, the hard soft thing.
Ask and the demon departs.

If I was a priest my homily
would be,
mavericks/minorities
we're Canaanites, we heard the rumours
there is always good wine in Cana and not just
at weddings.
We ask for faith and wine.
Demons have become technicalities.

– *Matthew* 15: 21–25

THE COMPLEX PAST THE DOOR
A LIFE OF JAMES LIDDY

Tyler Farrell

Louis Zukofsky wrote, "As a poet I have always felt that the work says all there needs to be said of one's life". This more than aptly fits when describing the life of James Liddy. If a reader of Liddy wants to discover James, all he needs to do is examine the poetry, the letters, the essays; and the short biographies at the back of poetry magazines, books and anthologies. Liddy's life is scattered in his extensive body of work. He was a generous person who invited many into his world. He lived long and, because he honoured youth, never became cynical. He worked hard at the conviction that poetry and the self were sacrosanct.

Who is James Liddy? Since James wrote many of his own biographical notes, as well as two late-life autobiographies, we can hear his voice and humour, feel his undying sense of art. Here is the small biographical note on the back cover of *A White Thought in a White Shade*, his first selected poems, published in 1987:

James Liddy was born on the night of the long knives and learnt to live in Dublin, Kilkee and Co. Wexford. He was educated by the monks at Glenstal, and by Patrick Kavanagh in McDaid's. He has taught in San Francisco, Portland, Galway, New York, New Orleans and is now Associate Professor of English at the University of Wisconsin-Milwaukee. Books of his poems have been published by the following presses: Dolmen, Humanities, Gotham Book Mart, The White Rabbit, hit & run, Capra and the Malton. A novella was brought out by the Wolfhound Press in 1985.

He would like to have been Baudelaire. He wishes to live someday in Mexico or Morocco. Ireland, a country of charmers instead of saints and poets instead of scholars, is a preparation for literature and other places.

There are many curious aspects to this brief note. First is the mention of "the night of the long knives", the purge which took place primarily on 1 July 1934, in which Hitler carried out many political executions, mostly on members of the Sturmabteilung or "brownshirts", in order to consolidate his power and send a message of complete command over the Nazi party. James used this coincidence to place himself inside history, to connect with a significant moment in European, indeed, world history. James loved connections to the timeline of the world and constantly talked of dates, times and places. It defined him and helped to create his voice. It ran throughout his poetry.

Another theme often included in Liddy's contributor notes is the almost continual mention of place, an Irish obsession perhaps. Liddy was born on Lower Pembroke Street in Dublin, and spent much time in Kilkee, Co. Clare (where his mother owned a house), and of course in Coolgreaney, Co. Wexford, where he grew up with his father (a dispensary doctor), mother, and sister Nora, who would later become a pediatrician and medical officer. There is often confusion with Liddy's place of birth. In some of his biographical notes, Liddy claims to have been born in Kilkee, while other writers have placed his birth in many places, including New York City, apparently confusing him with his mother. James could place his birth in different places, because for him birth was an imaginative event, not a geographical one. He was born often and in many places.

Liddy's first incarnation as a writer can be seen in the magazine *Arena* which he published (subsidized by his mother) and edited with Liam O'Connor, and later with Michael Hartnett as well. He would edit other magazines, but *Arena* was the first and probably the most influential, containing some of the last works of Patrick Kavanagh, and introducing new writers such as Leland Bardwell and Hartnett. And while the magazine was short lived (only four issues published from 1963–1965), it brought James to the world in grand style. His first book, *In a Blue Smoke* (Dolmen Press, 1964) came out shortly before *Arena* ended and was the start of Liddy's extensive literary career. As he writes in the introduction to *This Was Arena* (Malton Press reissue, 1982), "I have always wanted to exchange new magazines for old, for I know that magazines can alter the shape of a literary landscape". In Liddy's world, the literary landscape more than changed, it constantly evolved.

Throughout Liddy's life, he would continue to compulsively write and publish. His output, like his voice, increased and improved. "He never became soft", as he once wrote about fellow Irish poet Louis MacNeice. He added to his list of publishers by releasing poetry and memoir with Salmon and some of his most realized poetry with Arlen House. He also continued to produce and edit magazines of work by his friends and students in the form of *The Gorey Detail* and *The Blue Canary*. The former was published from 1977–1983 in a handful of issues in conjunction with Paul Funge's Gorey Arts Festival in Co. Wexford. The latter was published in many forms (postcards, T-shirts, pamphlets) from the 1990s until Liddy's death on 5 November 2008. *The Blue Canary* (named after a Milwaukee restaurant, now sadly gone) was a pet project of Liddy's with issues dedicated to Dickie Riordan and Lorine Niedecker and launches at various Milwaukee landmarks such as Valent's, a bar which opened at 6am for the Milwaukee industrial graveyard shift workers. *The Blue Canary* was a magazine for writers James respected, worked with and taught. Both of these magazines exhibit James at his best, most freely the poet, most himself. *The Gorey Detail* also contains quite humorous biographical information. "James Liddy: Barred from Neary's in 1974"; "James Liddy: Married April 25th, 1983, by the statues of Goethe and Schiller, Washington Park, Milwaukee". The poet creates himself, invents, and exaggerates.

James, the consummate poet, always held adoration for the nuanced self. It was important in much of his writing, whatever the genre. Here is another self-penned biographical note:

> James Liddy spent his early life in Dublin, amongst the poets. His latter years are sequestered in Milwaukee, not quite so literary a city! His selected poems are still available from Creighton University Press.

This was written for *Poets in a Frieze & A Valentine* published by the Poetry New York pamphlet series in 1999. Liddy's *Collected Poems* (Creighton University Press, 1994) was still quite new and James was proud, much like he was when a friend would write and congratulate him on its publication, or when he would give a graduate student money to purchase the book at a reading saying, with a smile, "That way I'll make a little commission". In referring to his *Collected* as a "selected", James was not making a mistake, but naming it more accurately. A complete collection, even in 1994, would be at least twice as long. Liddy's *Collected* represents, quite well, his major collections up to that point. However, there are small gaps in his choices, as if to say that there would be no possible way to "collect" all of James Liddy. James sent poems all over the world, felt that poems should be given away. He wrote and published often: small pamphlet poems in honour of Christmas, contributions to American and Irish magazines, interviews such as one with John Montague about John Berryman's reading in Dublin: "I was there. You were a ghost, and Yeats was a ghost, and John Berryman became a ghost shortly afterwards". He appears also in anthologies dedicated to poems about James Joyce, Patrick Kavanagh, Milwaukee and religion. He always wrote, often after returning from a night out with friends. Again, he pushed his writing to be better – the complex evolution of the poet and the self.

A more thorough and later personal account was written by James for Jessie Lendennie's anthology, *Salmon: A Journey in Poetry, 1981–2007* roughly a year before his death:

> James Liddy was born in the Pembroke nursing home in Dublin, a distinction he curiously shares with the author of a critical work on him, Brian Arkins. His parents hailed from Limerick and New York. He has lived in Wexford, Dublin, and the USA. While a UCD student he took his camera to the unveiling of a centenary plaque on Oscar Wilde's house opposite the church where his parents were married and he was baptised ...

Again, we see the history lesson, but more introspective this time. We read of the lineage of history and place, the link to the past. Or as James wrote in "I, The Poet", in the first issue of *Arena*, "the poet is an adult who is permitted by grace to relive in exploration his mysterious childhood. He does not repeat childhood; he restores it adventurously so he may find a human preparation for others – and for himself". As history moves, so does the poet.

Many small biographical notes also contain most of the necessary information: James' law degree from King's Inn in 1961, his admiration of Joyce and his job as second curator of the Martello Tower, his place in the late Irish Modernist movement, and his love for his adoptive dream city of Milwaukee: "A city of an impossible Germany, a possible Poland, and the vanishing Irish – plus the grail search for the most perfect bar in the world". Conversely, the parts of Liddy's life that are often missing from biographical notes are his influences, his ability to inspire and nurture young poets, his homosexuality, and most importantly, his antinomian Catholicism. We see some of these traits discussed in works like the Michael Begnal edited Festschrift, *Honeysuckle, Honeyjuice: A Tribute to James Liddy* (Arlen House, 2006) and in the concluding essays in four of the Arlen House poetry books. He mentions to Arkins in the critical study (Arlen House, 2001), "I will have to say straightaway that being queer, like being Irish and being Catholic, has charted my imagination". But his influences also appear in the form of writers and saints in poems and elsewhere: Baudelaire, Jack Spicer, George Moore, Kerouac, Joyce, Ginsberg, Woody Guthrie, Kavanagh, various popes (Pope John XXIII and Pope Benedict XV) and saints.

Many of Liddy's traits can be found while listening to his closest friends, people who experienced the encouragement, generosity, and respect of James. One of the most acute descriptions was written by a fellow poet and UW-Milwaukee colleague Jim Hazard, for the publication of *Radio X-Mas* (Blue Canary 2004):

> We're all God's children. But some are moreso. James Liddy is moreso.
>
> James comes to us from several more interesting places than this one: Dublin, New Orleans, San Francisco, among them. He is an advocate of gaiety, pub life, the solitude of reading, gossip, and the Milwaukee County bus system – Route 15 in particular.
>
> But these are not reasons he is God's child and moreso. James is a poet of radiant and saucy music. Etonnez-moi the old Russian tap dancer said, but to that stern dictum James adds poems that entertain us, make us dance, and help us to remember our prayers.

Perhaps the most telling mixture of James' intellect, love, and faith comes directly from his letters to students and friends, advising them to embrace what made them, to tap into a personal voice driving a writer to write, a singer to sing. Some advice on poetry, "Take only the complex past the door. You have to feast with panthers who have been to psychiatrists. There are achieved phrases. You are really working at excavating the core, a good deal of kraft, the art of poetry in Wisconsin; the poetry takes on smoothness. There is no final manuscript, only versions of what a poet might become". James wanted the poet to live, like him, through expressions of the soul and news of places to write about, new people with whom to discuss. "My friend, I write from the old Spain to your ghost in New Mexico. We had some extraordinary days in Grenada, with Ian Gibson, following the breath of Lorca, from orange tree to house to photos and letters. The poet is not dead! Yours, James". Also, in letters from Ireland, he spoke in epiphany, "Election Day here, European elections, no one understands Europe. The poll is low in America, but I love elections. Ancient Irish passion, long before democracy was invented. You will meet my Ireland when you come over. Not that it knows me much anymore". There was always an emotion to his letters, a personal voice and refreshing honesty. His letters are poems in themselves, inspiring and guiding.

James Liddy held devotion for poetry, friends, and life. His final days were spent in a hospital on the eastside of Milwaukee, visited by friends, people who loved him, wanted to thank him. His death reminds me of one more letter. The day after Michael Hartnett died in 1999 I had a lunch date with James at a favourite restaurant in Milwaukee. I was a fresh and inquisitive graduate student, a little drunk on beer, on poetry, on freedom, on new poems I had been working on. James was sad, "an angel in the deepest trench", he would say later. After lunch I thanked him on the doorstep of his Park Place apartment and went looking for Hartnett poems at Renaissance Books. In the dust of the lonely second floor poetry section, hidden between books unmoved in decades, I found *Anatomy of a Cliché* (Dolmen Press) Cost: $5. The next day I received a letter from James with a selection of Hartnett poems cut from an anthology. The note read:

> Dear Tyler, here are some poems from Hartnett's extensive works. Sorry if I was in bad form. I was really in inner mourning. Chunks of my Irish life are disappearing. Tomorrow, show me your poems – the gifts of dawn when they start to shine. With love, James.

Needless to say, I was hooked, grateful and enthralled with my new life. James strove to introduce students to his mind, his outlook, his wisdom. I was inspired and sat down to write a poem, something I hoped might impress the always complex and always loving poet, James Liddy.

Tyler Farrell's debut collection of poetry is *Tethered to the Earth* (Salmon Poetry, 2008).

About the Author

James Liddy was born in Lower Pembroke Street, Dublin, in 1934. His parents hailed from the cities of Limerick and New York. He lived in Coolgreany, Co. Wexford, intermittently from 1941 to 2000. His books include *In a Blue Smoke* (Dolmen, 1964), *Blue Mountain* (Dolmen, 1968), *A Munster Song of Love and War* (White Rabbit, 1971), *Baudelaire's Bar Flowers* (Capra/White Rabbit, 1975), *Corca Bascinn* (Dolmen, 1977), *Collected Poems* (Creighton UP, 1994), *Gold Set Dancing* (Salmon, 2000), and from Arlen House, *I Only Know that I Love Strength in My Friends and Greatness* (2003), *On the Raft with Fr. Roseliep* (2006), *Wexford and Arcady* (2008), *Askeaton Sequence* (2008), *Fest City* (2010), *It Swings from Side to Side* (2011) and *Rome That Heavenly Country* (2011).

He was a Professor in the English Department at the University of Wisconsin-Milwaukee for many years, where he taught creative writing and Irish and Beat literature. *James Liddy: A Critical Study* by Brian Arkins was published by Arlen House in 2001 and the widely acclaimed *Honeysuckle, Honeyjuice: A Tribute to James Liddy*, edited by Michael S. Begnal, appeared in 2006. The first volume of his memoir, *The Doctor's House: An Autobiography* was published by Salmon in 2004, with volume two, *The Full Shilling*, appearing in 2009.

James Liddy passed away on 5 November 2008 following a short illness.

About the Editor

John Redmond is a Senior Lecturer in Creative Writing at the University of Liverpool. He has written two books of poems, *Thumb's Width* (2001) and *MUDe* (2008).